Original title:
Through the Bedroom Window

Copyright © 2025 Creative Arts Management OÜ
All rights reserved.

Author: Aidan Marlowe
ISBN HARDBACK: 978-1-80587-198-9
ISBN PAPERBACK: 978-1-80587-668-7

Sighs of the Evening Breeze

A pillow fight in fading light,
Feathers dance like wild delight.
The cat stares, a regal queen,
As giggles echo, soft and keen.

Outside, the world begins to fade,
In silliness, our plans are laid.
A fortress built of sheets and dreams,
Where laughter spills like sunlight beams.

Under the Moon's Tender Watch

The clock ticks loud, a playful tease,
While shadows sway with evening's breeze.
In pajamas bright, we start to plot,
For midnight snacks that hit the spot.

With whispers soft, we craft our tales,
Of daring quests and singing whales.
The moon looks down, with gentle light,
On laughter shared—our hearts take flight.

Chasing the Silent Stars

We lay on floor like stars we chase,
Mapping dreams in a velvet space.
A soda pop to fuel the night,
As silly faces take their flight.

Outside, the crickets tune their song,
While dreams collide, they won't be long.
Forgotten toys in our escapade,
Become the treasure we've displayed.

Scenes Beyond the Veil

Peeking out at shadows deep,
While giggles tear the night from sleep.
With swishing capes and capricious hats,
Our world transforms—no room for bats!

A lantern's glow on secret schemes,
We bake up cookies from our dreams.
The night is young, the moon our friend,
In this adventure, smiles won't end.

Bated Breath of Anticipation

The curtains flutter with a sigh,
As the neighbors argue, oh my!
A cat on the windowsill prances,
While I wait for my chance, one glances.

The laundry flaps like a flag,
And I giggle at the dog's wag.
Expectations bubble, rise, and pop,
As the clock ticks, tick-tock, stop!

Captured Moments in the Frame

A squirrel steals a snack today,
I swear it winked and ran away.
The mailman drops his letters down,
And stumbles on a rogue plastic crown.

A dance-off starts with my reflection,
Fighting shadows in perfect direction.
Photogenic insects take their chance,
While I laugh at their clumsy dance.

Tides of Change at the Pane

Rain starts tapping like a tune,
While I ponder the life of a raccoon.
Puddles form like tiny pools,
As I giggle at my neighbors' rules.

Wind shifts, bringing giggles and sighs,
As birds parade in the cloudy skies.
Laughter leaks past the frame's edge,
Like a secret whispered by a hedge.

Reflections on a Canvas of Clouds

Clouds parade, a fluffy array,
Painting stories in shades of gray.
I shout as bright colors collide,
As a rainbow slips in for a ride.

Sunshine peeks, a cheeky fellow,
Dancing behind the curtains, hello!
My thoughts swirl in delightful streams,
While I dream absurd, silly dreams.

Echoes of Twilight Gleam

The cat leaps high with a mighty pounce,
While shadows dance like a lively ounce.
Outside the world wears a quirky hat,
A raccoon rummaging, chubby and fat.

Neighbors shout as they chase their dog,
While I sip tea, feeling like a hog.
The clock ticks loud, an unwelcome guest,
As squirrels plot their next crazy quest.

The Soft Breath of Dawn

Morning light peeks with a cheeky grin,
A bird starts singing, a tune to spin.
Coffee spills over the edge of the cup,
While the toast does a flip, oh what a pup!

The dog runs back with a sock in his mouth,
While the sun stretches wide, heading south.
A neighbor jogs, tripping on laces,
As laughter erupts in faraway places.

Chrysalis of Night's Solitude

The moon wears a crown of twinkling stars,
While we stay up trading stories from Mars.
A mouse darts by, with a slice of cheese,
Making midnight snacks feel like a breeze.

The clock strikes twelve, what a bizarre time,
A dance with shadows feels oh so prime.
My book falls closed, snoring starts to play,
Dreams dancing wildly, come what may.

Silhouettes of the Setting Sun

Colors melt as the sun takes a bow,
The world tilts up, what's funny right now?
A squirrel steals chips from the garden feast,
While laughter erupts, oh what a beast!

Friends gather round, telling tall tales,
About how the last pie met its gales.
The stars appear, like sprinkles on cake,
Making all of us giggle, chuckle, and shake.

Chasing Ephemeral Dreams

Bouncing balls on the sill, so near,
The cat on the ledge gives a sneer.
Pajamas fly as the wind takes a sweep,
While I chase my dreams caught in a heap.

Shoes on the roof, barking at stars,
Thought I spotted a cow, but it's just cars.
A froggy parade jumps to my tune,
Now who will guest star in this afternoon?

Under the blankets, the giggles collide,
With visions of pizza, I pop up in pride.
The moon winks and plays peek-a-boo,
While I toast my marshmallows to a sweet view.

Chasing shadows with laughter so bright,
My very own circus, each day a delight.
With dreams like balloons, ready to soar,
I'll snatch up the stars, who could want more?

A Chronicle of Light and Night

Whispers of twilight, the curtains a dance,
A glow from the streetlights, caught in a trance.
The dog pulls a prank and fakes a big snore,
While I giggle at socks that have long hit the floor.

Nudging the shadows, my teddy takes flight,
With a cape made of blankets, he's ready to fight.
Undercover heroes, they all have their dreams,
Swinging on chandeliers, bursting at the seams.

Cereal boxes hold secrets untold,
As I slurp on the milk, feeling brave and bold.
A midnight adventure in pajamas so bright,
To taste all the laughter that dances in light.

Chaos in corners where day meets the night,
With giggles and whispers, it's pure delight.
A tale spins onward, as bedtime descends,
Crafting a world where the fun never ends.

Whispers of the Morning Light

The sun peeks in, a cheeky grin,
As curtains dance, where mischief begins.
Coffee brews, the cat does prance,
A sleepy yawn, a morning dance.

Pajamas cling, a glorious sight,
Belly laughs brighten the dawn's light.
The toast pops up, we're off the hook,
Who knew mornings could be this good?

In this realm of playful haze,
We toss our woes in the sun's warm rays.
Tickling the moments with soft delight,
Oh, joy, how you bloom in morning light!

Secrets in the Curtain's Fold

Behind the fabric, whispers swirl,
A sock brigade, in chaos they twirl.
The dust bunnies schemed a wild affair,
While giggles burst like they just don't care.

The dog, with grace, leaps over the bed,
Chasing tails where secrets are fed.
In pillow forts, we dream up schemes,
Life's but a comedy stitched with dreams.

The world outside seems rich and bright,
But oh! the chaos behind the light.
With giggly hopes and snacks galore,
We find our joy and always want more.

Shadows at Dusk

The day dims down, shadows play tricks,
With silly shadows that wiggle and mix.
Silly faces on the wall they draw,
A dance of light that earns much guffaw.

Chasing giggles in the dusky air,
Footsteps echo, laughter to spare.
The world outside sighs and unwinds,
While giddy secrets are all that we find.

With snacks in hand, our squad convenes,
In twilight's glow, we plan grand scenes.
Round and round, the stories unfold,
In this kingdom of dusk, we are bold.

Melodies of the Night Sky

Under moonlight, the world feels sweet,
A serenade of chirps is our treat.
The stars take stage in sparkly suits,
As we prance about in our funky boots.

On the window's ledge, the cricket's hum,
Turns bedtime tales into a wild drum.
With giggles sprouting in twilight's embrace,
We're laughing shadows in our cozy space.

Dreams flit by like fireflies bright,
Collecting laughter into the night.
In our giggle fest under starlit skies,
Each note a treasure, each laugh a prize.

The Postcard of a Dream

In a slumber's embrace, a cat takes charge,
Chasing socks like fairies, oh how they enlarge.
The dreams start to dance, in colors so bright,
While the dog snores along, lost in the night.

The lamp flickers softly, casting shadows that prance,
Laughing at the curtains, inviting a chance.
A wardrobe of wonders, spilling clothes on the floor,
Each item a ticket to strange places galore.

A squirrel shimmies by, with a twitch of its tail,
Sending a postcard, a hilarious tale.
As laughter erupts, from a dreamscape divine,
The world outside calls, but this moment's just fine.

Moonlit Secrets

A spider spins tales in a web of delight,
Whispers of mischief, unseen in the night.
The starry-eyed moon paints silver on dreams,
While the floor creaks and giggles, or so it seems.

Under the blanket, the shadows do play,
Crafting funny images that wiggle away.
A lonely sock's doing the tango with flair,
As giggles turn silent, a secret to share.

The clock ticks with laughter, a thief in the dark,
Chasing time like a puppy, no sign of a bark.
Each flicker of light, a story untold,
Moonlit secrets unfold, both silly and bold.

The Lure of the Outside World

With a peek from the sill, the world seems so grand,
Freedom's sweet echo, adventures unplanned.
The garden's a jungle, wild and alive,
Where dandelions dance, and mischief will thrive.

A frog leaps and croaks, a comedic duet,
Waving to a bee, no sign of regret.
The clouds wear a grin, floating high in the sky,
As birds throw a party, their tunes flying by.

Yet inside it's a circus of pillows and fluff,
The old cat is plotting, her patience is tough.
A tug on the curtain, a battle of wills,
Who'll win the great showdown? It's time for the thrills!

Narratives in a Quiet Corner

In a quiet nook, where the dust bunnies dwell,
A tale spins carefully, like a mischievous spell.
The lamp plays a game, casting shadows of glee,
As the cat and the sock puppet plot a decree.

A notebook unfolds, with doodles and dreams,
Each line tells a story, or so it seems.
The chair creaks with laughter, a wise old sage,
While the teddy bear chuckles, flipping a page.

The world spins away, but here it's a blast,
With whispers of memories, sweet moments amassed.
In this nook of silence, where laughter ignites,
Narratives flourish, in playful delights.

Kaleidoscope of Seasons

Leaves dance in the wind just like a clown,
Socks mismatch, they tumble down.
Snowflakes turn into cotton candy fluff,
Winter's greet is never tough.

Sunshine pokes through curtains wide,
A bird on a branch, what a goofy ride!
Summer sun makes everyone sweat,
Caught in a towel, what a sight to get!

Autumn whispers with a chuckle,
Pumpkin hats that make us buckle.
Spring blooms with a playful tease,
Bumblebees buzzing, dancing with ease.

In the kaleidoscope of life we play,
Colors swirl in a funny ballet.
Each season giggles, takes its bow,
We laugh at their antics, here and now.

Reflections of a Life Unfolding

Mirrors argue, do they sway?
Tangled hair leads me astray.
Chasing shadows, what's the score?
I trip on laughter, want some more.

In each corner, jokes appear,
Reflections wink, they shift, they leer.
Coffee spills in silly glee,
Life is clumsy, can't you see?

Dancing alone with mismatched socks,
The dog joins in, we're in a paradox.
Moments in chaos become a song,
This wobbly ride can't be wrong!

Smiles are lingering like a sweet tune,
Joy spills over like a big balloon.
In the mirror's tales, we find our grace,
With every laugh, we embrace our place.

Horizons at the Break of Day

Sunrise giggles as it wakes,
Coffee brews and my stomach aches.
Birds belt tunes in a quirky choir,
Stretching wings, desires on fire!

Socks left behind, out on the street,
Running late, oh, isn't that neat?
A rabbit hops, gives a cheeky glance,
We both laugh, it's a funny dance.

Horizons blush in a silly hue,
Daytime's antics bring something new.
The sun trips over the cloud's big toe,
And everyone chuckles, don't you know?

Joyful moments in a raucous play,
Each dawn brings its own array.
In this circus of life, we sway,
Finding humor in the light of day.

The Colors of Solace

Crayons burst in a silly riot,
Doodles dance, oh, isn't it a riot?
Hues mingle like friends at a feast,
When laughter arises, worries cease.

Rainbows tiptoe across the sky,
Chasing a cloudy hat, oh my!
A sunny smile, a cheeky grin,
Colors spill out, where to begin?

Paint splatters tell tales so wild,
Canvas laughing like a child.
In strokes of joy, we color the day,
With every giggle, fears fade away.

Soft colors brush against our hearts,
Finding solace as whimsy imparts.
In this vibrant canvas, we mend,
A tapestry of laughter, around the bend.

The Lattice of Daybreak

Morning light peeks slyly in,
Cats dance, chasing shadows thin.
Coffee steams, a comical sight,
As the toast jumps in a playful fight.

Birds squawk tales of mischief made,
The dog dreams big, a runaway parade.
Socks on the lawn, a colorful sprawl,
Giggling children, a fun-loving squall.

Hats worn sideways, mismatched shoes,
Wild antics echo, breaking the snooze.
In this chaos, life finds its tune,
Where laughter reigns, morning's cartoon.

Neighbors peek, with raised brows high,
Wondering how the day passed by.
With every quirk, a smile so bright,
In the lattice of day, everything's right!

Shattered Reflections

In the mirror, a frown unfolds,
Pajama pants, a sight that boldly scolds.
Hair a nest, a bird could thrive,
Yet in this, I feel so alive.

Underneath the glamour of dawn,
Kitchen antics, the green smoothie's gone!
Splatters of yogurt, a sneaky attack,
Can my breakfast really fight back?

Dogs wear capes made of bedsheets bright,
Heroes of chaos, ready to fight.
And there's a sock in the butter dish,
Remnants of dreams, a funny wish.

Laughter blurs the lines of regret,
Life's a sitcom, you can bet.
With every flaw, the mirror's so grand,
In shattered reflections, we take a stand!

Outside the Veil of Sleep

Slippery floors and missing keys,
Mismatched slippers leave quiet pleas.
A puppet show from the laundry pile,
Each sock a character, unique with style.

Pancakes flip with a flurry of cheer,
While wet dog shakes bring giggles near.
Chasing the teen, who avoids the glare,
A trail of cereal lingers in the air.

Balloons in the garden, floating so high,
A cat in the mix, oh my oh my!
The mailman laughs, it's quite a scene,
As sleepyheads giggle at the routine.

Outside the veil, where dreams collide,
Every mishap is a fun-filled ride.
With laughter echoing in morning's embrace,
Life's little quirks find their place!

Gazing at the Horizon's Edge

Sunrise sneaks past the curtain's fold,
Breaking day with a joke retold.
The toaster pops like a circus act,
While the kettle sings, what's the next fact?

Kids burst forth with giggles galore,
Socks in the garden, that's for sure.
A runaway plant makes a break for the street,
As neighbors chuckle at this morning treat.

Chairs stacked high, a tower of fun,
Where breakfast ideas are never done.
With every spill, there's room for delight,
Gazing at antics, morning's delight.

Horizon lit with a colorful mishap,
Moments strung together in a nap-time wrap.
In laughter we find the joy we pledge,
As we gaze at life from its playful edge.

Glimmers of Dawn

The sun peeks in with a cheerful grin,
Chasing away dreams where snoring begins.
Tickles of light dance on my face,
While I pretend to be lost in space.

A cat stretches wide on the windowsill,
Eyeing the world with a majestic thrill.
Birds chime in with an off-key tune,
As I yawn, drifting back to the moon.

My pillow whispers, "Stay here awhile,"
But those rays shout, "Come join the smile!"
The world is a circus, so join the show,
Just don't forget to tie up your toe.

Coffee brews with a startling pop,
While my thoughts race to catch up and stop.
With each giggle sneaking through the cracks,
I leap from my nest, ready for laughs and snacks.

Chasing Shadows at Twilight

The sun bows low, painting skies so bright,
As shadows stretch and dance in twilight.
A squirrel plots mischief, tail held high,
While pigeons hold court and gossip nearby.

Flickering lights turn on, one by one,
Illuminating battles of day and fun.
I glimpse a raccoon with an acorn stash,
Eyes wide with wonder, I watch in a flash.

The evening breeze whispers funny tales,
About sock-stealing ghouls and wind-blown sails.
As giggles echo off walls so near,
I laugh at the antics that dance in the clear.

In this nightly show, I'm front-row seat,
With popcorn dreams and mismatched feet.
As stars appear, I take a deep breath,
Giggling with shadows, playing with jest.

Whispered Secrets beyond the Glass

A breeze comes floating, soft and sly,
Carrying secrets from the sky.
Curtains flutter in playful jest,
As I lean in for the nightly quest.

The moon grins wide, a curious friend,
Listening close as conversations blend.
Frogs croak symphonies, crickets hum,
Each sound a mystery we become.

Glimpses of life from a distance away,
Neighbors tease as babies play.
The world is a pageant, silly and sweet,
A kaleidoscope where oddities meet.

With each whispered word, I chuckle in glee,
As shadows prance and twirl with me.
This magic hour wrapped in delight,
Holds every secret, through day and night.

Sighs of Morning Light

Light spills in with a giggling glow,
Poking at dreams that don't want to go.
A cup of cheer sits by my side,
As the morning plays its playful ride.

The dog snores loud, a thunderous sound,
While the wind serenades with a swirl around.
I stretch my arms, embracing the air,
In this silly dance, I just can't care.

Bouncing socks stash stories untold,
As I spy on adventures of young and old.
Each shadow winks, each glimmer beams,
Inviting me back to my giggliest dreams.

So here I sit, with laughter on hold,
Gathering warmth as the world unfolds.
This morning's a riddle, wrapped up in light,
With sighs and snickers, it feels just right.

A Glimpse into the Uncharted

Peeking out while still in bed,
The garden gnomes, now fully fed.
Squirrels serenade, a morning show,
With acorns flying, off they go.

Clouds parade in silly shapes,
A dragon roars, and a monkey capes.
Sunbeams dance on the window sill,
Reflecting laughter, a gentle thrill.

Oh! What mischief in the air,
An invisible cat creeps with flair.
Bouncing shadows, a playful chase,
In this place, there's never disgrace.

Who's that waving, is it a ghost?
Or just my neighbor, buttered toast?
In this view, the world's a jest,
With each new dawn, a merry quest.

Fantasies in Fleeting Light

The sun spills gold on the quilted bed,
While fantasies bounce in my sleepy head.
Continents drift on a sea of dreams,
Full of giggles, and soft moonbeams.

Butterflies plotting a tiny parade,
With rainbow sprinkles in the shade.
A jester tumbles, laughter flows,
Chasing fairies, see how it goes!

Sudden visitors from afar,
A talking cat in a car, bizarre.
Whispers of magic on a breeze,
Tickling my toes, oh what a tease!

Clouds wear hats, and birds will waltz,
The world's full of giggles and no faults.
In fleeting light, what shall we see?
A daydream party, just you and me.

A Gateway to Reverie

Tiny portals to the unknown,
Open wide with a playful tone.
Donkeys in ties, a ballet troupe,
Twirling by in a cheerful group.

The neighbor's dog, a lookout keen,
In shades he lounges, looking serene.
While pancakes flip from the kitchen stave,
A breakfast feast, on a wave, we rave.

Glittering wishes hang on high,
Like rows of sausages, oh my!
A magical realm unfolds anew,
With silly shenanigans to pursue.

Behind the glass, the world's a jest,
Unruly laughter is always best.
In this realm of silly delight,
Every moment is a playful flight.

The Allure of New Horizons

While sunlight spills, the curtains sway,
A pirate ship sails on a whimsical bay.
With parrots that squawk the news of old,
And treasures of jellybeans, bright and bold.

Each gaze outside, a chance to play,
Imaginary friends join in the fray.
A circus rolls by, with elephants too,
On bicycles, wearing hats of blue.

Kites take flight on giggles' might,
With teddy bears flying to dizzying heights.
New horizons beckon with laughter's grace,
Promising joy in this wondrous space.

Amidst the chirps and morning breeze,
Life's a comedy that aims to please.
With every glance, the mundane falls away,
New adventures beckon at the break of day.

Vignettes of a Wandering Mind

A cat jumps high, a bird flies low,
I spill my coffee, watch it flow.
The clock ticks loud, yet I'm on pause,
Inventing tales with no real cause.

My socks are mismatched, funny and rare,
Invisible friends sit in my chair.
I dance in slippers, twirl around,
The dog just stares, in silence, renowned.

Outside the world spins, cars zoom by,
While I'm tangled in sheets, sighing why.
The neighbor's garden grows weeds so tall,
Yet I'm the one who can't stand at all.

In my head, there's a silent parade,
Of cartoons dancing in a grand charade.
With giggles and snaps, they pop and burst,
In this odd sanctuary, I overly thirst.

The Color of Stillness

Sunlight streams, but I'm still in bed,
Dreaming of toast, but I see no bread.
Outside the laughter trips on the lawn,
While I ponder if pajamas are still on.

A sock puppet show with no one to see,
The shadow of me laughing wildly at tea.
Painted on walls are stories untold,
Colors of mischief in laughter unfold.

Birds chirp loudly as I munch on chips,
Creating grand speeches without any quips.
The curtains sway in a breezy debate,
With whispers of chaos, and oh, what a fate!

In silent mirth, the hours go round,
I'm cloaked in a realm where silliness found.
Every tick of the clock's a punchline anew,
In this quiet stillness, I'm clearly askew.

Explorations of the Midnight Hour

Nights are wild when the world's asleep,
Monsters in closets, secrets to keep.
I tiptoe softly, a ninja in socks,
Sneaking for snacks among the old clocks.

The fridge hums gently, a tale of its own,
Leftover pizza, oh how it's grown!
I dance with shadows, play tag with the past,
While emails and to-do lists wait, unsurpassed.

The moon beams bright, a mischievous grin,
She winks at the chaos, inviting the spin.
Wall art takes shape, becomes a friend,
As thoughts converge safely, round every bend.

In midnight's embrace, I giggle aloud,
The clock rolls its eyes, oh how I'm proud.
In this kingdom of night, dreams intertwine,
Explorations unending, like silly, sweet wine.

Reflections of a Quiet Desire

In the mirror's glance, who do I see?
A champion of daydreams, wild and free.
With a wink of the eye and a nod of the head,
I scribble sweet wishes from my cozy bed.

Pillows hear secrets, they always agree,
With mischief and laughter, just let it be.
The world could be chaos, but here it's a rhyme,
As I shuffle through moments, not bound by time.

In corners, the dust bunnies hold a debate,
Trading old stories, deciding my fate.
The light flickers softly, a gentle muse,
In quiet reflection, what shall I choose?

To chase after giggles or solidify dreams,
My heart dances lightly, bursting at seams.
In stillness, I spark, like a comet in flight,
In this cozy retreat, everything feels right.

New Beginnings Beyond the Threshold

I see the world in my pajamas,
Sipping coffee with mismatched socks.
Birds are chirping like comedians,
While squirrels hold acorn stocks.

The sun spills in like a clumsy friend,
Tripping over furniture, delighting the room.
My plans long gone, I can only pretend,
To embrace this absurd little gloom.

Neighbors dance in their yard's limelight,
One's still in PJs, eyeing my toast.
They don't know that I've turned polite,
While bursting with laughter, it'd be a roast!

But here I sit, all snuggled in peace,
A grin on my face, like a Cheshire cat.
Every silly moment seems to increase,
As life's little folly is where it's at!

Stars that Entertain the Imagination

Time creeps by as I gaze outside,
Those twinkling gems in the darkened sky.
I name each star, like a secret guide,
But my dog's barking makes me sigh.

He thinks they're aliens—what a surprise!
Jumping and howling, he claims to know,
While I ponder how dreamy the night implies,
Imagining worlds where UFOs could flow.

Each flicker a joke, each comet a laugh,
The moon winks, sharing a cosmic jest.
With popcorn in hand, I grab a whole half,
As the universe sprawls its nightly fest.

So here I sit, with my wacky perspective,
Wondering what mysteries stars might gift.
In a world of night, so vast and reflective,
I drift on dreams, letting laughter lift.

Echoes of Unsaid Words

Silent thoughts bounce off the walls,
Whispered secrets dance in the air.
The cat stares on, as gravity calls,
While I debate what's fair or unfair.

My sock drawer is a dictionary wide,
Of all the half-spoken things I've lost.
Each pair a memory, or a silent guide,
Keeping chaos at bay, counting the cost.

An echo may shout what I can't declare,
Like my plants stretching toward the sun.
Fronds waving wildly like they don't care,
In this dilemma, who's really having fun?

So I'll laugh at the silence, the stories unspun,
With echoes lingering where words did hide.
In this cozy room, I've nowhere to run,
Just the humor left in a whispering tide.

Adventures Behind the Glass

Peeking out, it's a wild parade,
Socks and shoes on the neighboring line.
Tiny adventures, like a charade,
Frogs in formation, passing the time.

A raccoon rummages with a sly finesse,
While birds gossip like they own the street.
Nature's comedy, I must confess,
Becomes quite a show, oh what a treat!

The rain dances forth like a lively dance,
Each drop a character with a tale to tell.
Even clouds swirl in a whimsical trance,
As if they could break out of their shell.

So I stay glued, with a chuckle in hand,
Watching the world through my glassy frame.
In each tiny scene, I make my own brand,
In this stage set up, nothing's too tame!

Memory's Canvas in the Sunlight

The cat sprawls wide, a pillow of fur,
As I wrestle with thoughts, a mere blur.
Outside, kids tumble, laughter ablaze,
While I sip my tea, lost in a daze.

A neighbor's dog barks a high-pitched song,
Breaking the silence where I don't belong.
Sunlight paints dust in a golden ballet,
Snores fill the air, come join the café!

Footsteps parade across the old floor,
My socks slide and skid, crash into the door!
Mirrors chuckle at my ungraceful flight,
This life's a circus, oh what a delight!

Memory's hues blend, a splash of fun,
With a wink and a smile, just barely begun.
Timeless adventures whirl in the rays,
As I twirl in my mind during lazy days.

Veils of Time and Tranquility

Shadows dance softly in the fading light,
While I plot my escape from this cozy plight.
Chips on the table, soda bubbles burst,
As I listen to time, in laughter immersed.

The clock ticks away, a whimsical beat,
A jester in disguise, never discreet.
Whispers of tomorrow tickle my ear,
As I spill popcorn, I've nothing to fear!

Rain taps gently against the old pane,
It's a symphony played, with no disdain.
Clothes dance on hangers, caught in a tease,
This life is a comedy, put me at ease!

Veils of the past flutter, giggles unfold,
The stories of laughter and joy yet untold.
Each moment a treasure, a lighthearted rhyme,
In this cozy nook, I'm a partner to time.

The Poetry of a Silent Night

Moonlight spills secrets on evening's deep cloth,
As I search for snacks in the bright light froth.
A midnight dance, the fridge is my muse,
With every crunch, I can hardly choose!

The neighbor's TV blares a silly show,
While I giggle alone, a shadowy glow.
Whispers of dreams float past sleepy sighs,
As I muse on my life in pajama disguise.

Socks mismatched, a fashion disaster,
Yet here, in my lair, I'm the brightmaster!
Tickling the night with my chuckles and cheer,
In silence so loud, I hold laughter near.

Poetry flows when the world's feeling meek,
In this sanctuary, I'm unabashedly sleek.
Tomorrow will come, with its chaos and fright,
But tonight, I'm a queen in the glow of moonlight.

Fluttering Hearts Meet the Wind

A breeze whispers secrets, flutters a smile,
While I sit on my bed, all tangled in style.
The curtains sway wildly, a ballet of glee,
As the world outside laughs, 'Come dance with me!'

Balloons drift by, drawn by the sun,
With every little giggle, my heart's come undone.
In this cozy retreat, all silliness thrives,
Tickles and chuckles are the joy that derives.

My sandwich steals bites while I can't turn around,
The toast's jumping jacks make a playful sound.
Dare I laugh harder? Oh, why not try!
The fluttering hearts soar, oh my, oh my!

Tick-tock of laughter, like chimes in the breeze,
This nonsensical rhythm sets my mind at ease.
Let's sip from the cup of ridiculous bliss,
In this world made of joy, how could I resist?

Secrets Nestled in Draped Curtains

A cat plots mischief with a gaze so sly,
Whiskers twitching, as birds flit by.
The curtain sways with her secret dreams,
While shadows dance, or so it seems.

In laughter's hush, the sunlight peeks,
Picking up whispers, the curtain sneaks.
Moments of chaos wrapped in thread,
As socks hide snugly where kittens tread.

The Dance of Leaves at Dusk

Outside the pane, the leaves take flight,
In a tango, swirling, oh what a sight!
An acorn tumbles with a mighty thud,
While squirrels critique from their leafy bud.

Each rustle gasps like a breathless roar,
As critters ponder and raccoons explore.
Twilight giggles, the stars begin to peek,
Nature's show for the well-dressed cheek.

Faded Footsteps on Morning Dew

The dew drops giggle on blades so green,
With footprints trailing, left unseen.
A wayward pet trots on a quest,
Seeking crumbs in a morning jest.

Each step a whisper, a clumsy beat,
Nature's jesters patter on their feet.
The sun peeks in, it gives a nudge,
As laughter spills in a gentleudge.

Palette of Life Beyond the Sill

The flower pot winks in colors bright,
As bugs pose models in evening light.
A painter spilled hues onto the grass,
While daisies chuckle as they pass.

Beanstalks wiggle like they're full of fun,
Swaying proudly in the setting sun.
Each bloom a joke, each petal a grin,
In a colorful world, let the giggles begin!

Fragments of Daybreak

The rooster crows, a start so bright,
My coffee spills, oh what a sight!
A cat leaps high, a graceful show,
While my slippers dance toe to toe.

A squirrel scrambles, makes me jump,
Chasing shadows, a playful thump.
Sunlight creeps, it winks and glows,
As I trip on my own two toes.

The neighbor's dog has found his bark,
In pajamas, I wander in dark.
With laughter shared, we greet the dawn,
A circus act, our day moves on.

With every call and every chime,
The world outside, it feels like rhyme.
As day unfolds, we smile and play,
In morning light, we find our way.

Reflections on the Sill

Perched on soft, the kittens lie,
With sleepy eyes and a long sigh.
Birds outside have much to say,
As I join them in my own way.

I watch the leaves, a dance so funny,
They shimmy well, oh, aren't they sunny?
A dog on wheels rolls down the street,
It's quite the sight, oh what a feat!

A neighbor sneezes, oh, what a roar!
The flowers giggle at the door.
I sip my tea, the world's a show,
With each small peep, new stories flow.

The sun takes center stage above,
Warming hearts, like a big hug.
With every glance, the laughter spills,
Reflections pure, on the sunny sills.

A Gaze into the Outside

I peer outside at the busy lane,
A squirrel dances, what a brain!
In shiny shoes, the mailman prances,
While kids play tag, and fate romances.

A bicycle bell rings out with cheer,
As ice cream trucks draw near and near.
A pigeon struts like he's the king,
While all around, the joy winds spring.

Mismatched socks on a neighbor's line,
A fashion choice that is quite divine!
With every giggle that fills the air,
The outside world dances without care.

I can't help but join in the fun,
The quiet world soon becomes a run.
And with each glance, my laughter grows,
In this bright light, anything goes.

The Quiet Eye of the Room

The chair reclines, a cozy throne,
While dust motes waltz in light well-known.
A pair of socks just shyly peek,
Daring the floor to take a leap.

The clock ticks loud in perfect rhyme,
While my tea goes cold, oh such a crime!
A moth decides to take its flight,
Around my head, what a silly sight!

The cushions giggle as I sit,
With scattered toys that seem to flit.
Each corner whispers secrets fair,
In every nook, there's joy to share.

Soon the cat will join the game,
As laughter loops like an old refrain.
In the quiet eye, the room will bloom,
With smiles that dance and dreams that zoom.

The Scent of Boundless Possibilities

In the morning light so bright,
A cat outside plots his flight.
He sees a bird, thinks he's sly,
With a leap, he aims for the sky.

Coffee brews with joyful cheer,
While socks are found, oh my dear!
A dance of clothes upon the floor,
What treasures lie behind the door?

The neighbor's dog seems to bark,
As I watch his sill, the world's a lark.
Each glance reveals a new delight,
In this comedy of morning light.

Suddenly, the mailman slips,
Tripping on his own two trips.
The world outside, a crazy scene,
In the quiet, I laugh unseen.

Embrace of the Northern Lights

A glow outside, it pulls me near,
With colors dancing, bright and clear.
The cat meows, a curious smile,
Wonders if it's worth the while.

The snowflakes fall in swirling spree,
As I sip on my cup of tea.
Lights flicker like a playful sprite,
Turning the dark into pure delight.

A squirrel hops from branch to branch,
Thinking life is one big dance.
With winter's chill, we find our fun,
Here's to joy, each day begun!

With laughter shared through window frame,
Who knew the night would look this same?
In a world that seems so bright,
We find our reason to take flight.

The Story Beyond the Solid Frame

What tales reside right outside my glass?
With passing cars and folks that pass.
That awkward jogger slips on a shoe,
And off he goes, a dash askew!

A child rides by on a tricycle,
His laughter rings, it's quite a miracle.
While birds debate what seeds to steal,
Nature's show, it's quite the reel!

The old bike shop, its door ajar,
A mystery wrapped in a rusty car.
Each glimpse a glimpse, a giggle's call,
In this world, there's fun for all.

The neighbor waves with an ice cream cone,
As I ponder tales of my own.
Life outside, a comic strip,
With humor wrapped in each little trip.

Ruminations of a Restless Soul

Nighttime whispers, the moon is bright,
As I peer out, what a funny sight!
An owl hoots, giving me a wink,
"Is that a rabbit, or just a blink?"

With crickets chirping a lively tune,
The stars above feel like a balloon.
A raccoon sneaks into the scene,
What mischief now, oh so keen!

My cat's eyes dart, filled with glee,
"What lies beyond? Come, just see!"
A world where shadows play and race,
In every corner, a silly face.

Each night reveals a new delight,
A silly dance beneath the light.
Ruminations of joy, they swirl,
In this restless heart, a playful twirl.

Framed Reminiscence

In the morning light I peek,
A cat's tail flicks, she's on the sneak.
Dust bunnies dance in playful rows,
While my old sock gives off a pose.

Birds are chirping, what a scene,
Squirrels plotting, oh so keen.
My neighbor's dance breaks all the rules,
Swatting bees like jesting fools.

Trees wave gently, hats askew,
A raccoon dreams of a morning brew.
Sunshine winks, while I just sigh,
Is that a donut I spy nearby?

Each moment frames a laugh or two,
Life's a circus in vibrant hue.
With every glance, new stories bloom,
My silly world, all busy in the room.

Dreams Reflecting in Stillness

A bunny hops, it seems so sly,
Leaping past with a winked eye.
Rain on glass, it plays a tune,
Who knew drips could make you swoon?

Clouds drift in, just like a show,
Critters gather, all in a row.
Tails swish and wiggle, what a sight,
A dog dreaming of his next big bite.

From sill to sill, the shadows chase,
The wind sings softly, a cotton lace.
A butterfly lands for a quick blitz,
Tickling bugs as they throw their fits.

In the stillness, giggles arise,
As mismatched socks take to the skies.
Colors swirl in joy-filled flight,
I chuckle softly at this delight.

Night's Embrace beneath Starry Veils

With twilight's brush, the world slows down,
A raccoon dons a silly frown.
Moonbeams bounce on rooftops bright,
As owls share tales of furry fright.

Shadows dance on sleepy walls,
Whispers echo through the halls.
The cat snickers at a ghost,
While I partake in midnight toast.

Bats dart by, their furry tricks,
Mice giggle, doing funny flips.
In soft embrace of midnight hues,
I stifle laughter at silly moods.

Under this blanket of the night,
Reality mixes with dream's delight.
Each twinkling star holds a silly tale,
As nighttime chuckles begin to sail.

Echoes of Distant Laughter

From the porch, the world seems grand,
Tiny feet with muddy hand.
A kite goes up, then takes a dive,
A glimpse of joy, I feel alive.

In gardens where the flowers giggle,
Bees buzzing, oh, they wiggle.
Hiccups from a laughing pie,
Neighbors wave and sigh goodbye.

Each window frames a funny face,
A grandma's wig falls from its place.
Laughter echoes through the air,
Bringing warmth like sunshine's glare.

As stars peek in with brighter cheer,
The world's a stage, so filled with cheer.
Each whispered joke, a special gift,
In this wild life, we all uplift.

The Quietude of Soft Rain

Pitter-patter on the panes,
A symphony of small complaints,
As raindrops dance like little sprites,
They hum their tunes through cozy nights.

My cat's confusion peaks anew,
As he thinks that clouds are squirrels too,
He leaps and bounds, a sight to see,
In this wet wonderland, he's so free.

With every drip, a giggle draws,
As socks conspire with puddly paws,
I chuckle softly, life's a jest,
When rainstorms visit, we feel blessed.

Water's ballet on the sill,
Seems to charm my daily thrill,
As clouds parade and kids delight,
In playful puddles, hearts take flight.

Fragments of a Beloved Dream

In slumber's grip, I roam afar,
With marshmallow clouds as my bizarre car,
I bump into a talking chair,
Who asks if I've seen its missing pair.

A fish in a tux, he starts to sing,
About how he forgot his bling,
With laughter bubbling in my soul,
This dreamy world makes me feel whole.

The clock's awake, but I'm still not,
Dancing with shadows, I call my spot,
My shoes made of cheese, they squeak and squeal,
In this funny dream, everything feels real.

Awoken by giggles, my cat takes flight,
Chasing illusions that fade from sight,
Yet in my heart, the fragments gleam,
As I ponder the silliness of the dream.

When the World Breaths Outside

The world exhales in bursts of cheer,
As crickets chirp, I pause to hear,
The breeze tells jokes, a gentle tease,
While leaves perform their funny lease.

Clouds wear hats of fluffy delight,
Bobbing around in whimsical flight,
Children laugh, as puddles splash,
In every drop, a tender laugh.

A dog with socks, he struts on by,
With tongue out ready, he aims for the sky,
As ants in their suits march in a line,
A picnic awaits, all just divine.

The sun winks golden from the sky,
As butterflies flutter, oh my, oh my,
With nature's giggles all around,
In this comical world, joy is found.

Murmurs of an Unseen Garden

Behind the curtain, sneaky gnomes,
Whisper of their leafy homes,
With grins so wide, they plot and scheme,
In a world where flowers dream.

The daisies gossip, point and jest,
At the busy bees who never rest,
While tulips wear the latest styles,
And humor blooms for endless miles.

A pumpkin chuckles, round and spry,
Swaying gently as butterflies fly,
The sunflowers wave with silly flair,
In this garden, joy fills the air.

As shadows stretch and day turns night,
The critters join for a laugh-filled fright,
In this unseen realm, laughter grows,
In the murmurs of nature, happiness flows.

Daydreams and Distant Shores

In my head, I sail away,
On cardboard boats and bits of hay.
The ocean's jokes always run dry,
As seagulls perch and ask me why.

Pineapple hats and flip-flop shoes,
Dance with waves, I cannot lose.
They throw me fish, I toss back sand,
And laugh like dolphins, isn't it grand?

My anchor's wrapped in fluffy fluff,
Sailing's easy when seas are rough.
With ice cream sails and jellyfish,
I chart my course, and that's the wish!

So if you hear that giggle loud,
It's just my ship, lost in a cloud.
On distant shores where I pretend,
The waves are my most trusty friend.

Veils of Time and Light

In the morning, socks dance bright,
Shadows play hide and seek with light.
Tick-tock clocks are out for fun,
As time slips by—oh, what a run!

A waltz with dust, my dance partner,
Spins in circles, never a martyr.
I wear my watch on my shoe,
To track the time—who knows what's true?

Moments flutter like paper planes,
Soaring high, then down like chains.
I catch them quick, they giggle, flee,
And whisper secrets just for me.

At dusk, the stars roll out their mats,
While sleepy clouds wear sleepy hats.
The night's a trickster, full of glee,
And wraps the day in mystery.

Tapestry of Falling Leaves

Leaves tumble down, a twirling spree,
Whispers of autumn, wild and free.
Squirrels gather in a rush,
While acorns roll and try to hush.

Crisp jackets giggle in the breeze,
As branches sway and dance with ease.
A pumpkin winks, demands attention,
While footballs fly, a soft invention.

Color palettes blaze and blend,
Each leaf a letter, each curve a bend.
I weave them in a fancy hat,
And dance, surprised, at how I spat!

O autumn, your mosaic so bright,
Leaves catch laughter, filled with light.
They swirl like confetti, oh what fun,
My tapestry grows, and it's just begun!

Lanterns of Lost Moments

I hang my lanterns from the sky,
To find the hours that slipped by.
They flicker, giggle, say "Remember?"
As fireflies join the funny member.

I chase after time, with a net so wide,
Catching giggles, oh what a ride!
Each lost moment a glowing spark,
That dances brightly in the dark.

They tell me tales of dog and cat,
Of hats that fit and don't fall flat.
A comedy show, each twinkling light,
Makes the past shine oh-so-bright.

So here I stand, with lanterns raised,
Among the silliness, I'm amazed.
Each flick of memory, bright and bold,
Tells stories of laughs, forever told.

Canvas of a Thursday Dream

The curtains flutter, a dance on air,
A squirrel's acrobatics, quite the affair.
It steals my snacks like a thief in the night,
I laugh and I ponder, what a comical sight.

A cat on the sill, in a regal pose,
Dreaming of kingdoms, while striking a nose.
A playful pounce, and a leap so absurd,
I giggle, he stumbles - this scene's too stirred.

The paint smudged canvas, a masterpiece born,
As neighbors parade with their wild lawn decor.
In one yard, a flamingo, the next a giraffe,
I chuckle just thinking - who's got the last laugh?

Thursday afternoons, a whimsical spree,
Life's little antics, the show just for me.
A watching observer, in laughter I bask,
What day is more funny? I dare you to ask!

Threads of Twilight's Embrace

As twilight tiptoes and colors entwine,
The shadows play tag, on my wall they recline.
A raccoon in slippers, oh what a delight,
Raiding the bins, in the soft fading light.

The neighbor's loud rooster begins his grand song,
A misplaced alarm clock - the timing is wrong.
As I sip my tea, what a perplexing joy,
A chorus of chaos, like a bright, silly ploy.

An owl rolls his eyes at the antics below,
While I snicker and giggle, how funny they flow.
In nature's own theater, each show is a gem,
A quirky vignette, directing the mayhem.

Evening whispers secrets in laughter so sweet,
With moments like these, life's an amusing treat.
So I hold my breath, for the next tease ahead,
And smile at the mischief right under my bed!

Flight of the Sleepy Winds

The sleepy winds sigh as they wiggle and whirl,
Telling the tales of a dreaming world.
A lone sock floats by, oh what a parade,
In this nighttime circus, not a tally is made.

Hats on cat heads, who'd craft such a sight?
She blinks with disdain, "Not tonight, silly light."
The dog spins in circles, chasing his tail,
While I chuckle softly at this nightly detail.

A curtain's burst open as breeze takes a leap,
With giggles and tickles, the moon starts to creep.
Stockings on windows, a fashion so grand,
I'm left in stitches at this sight, quite unplanned.

The world outside giggles, a frolicsome mate,
In windswept adventures, we roll and we skate.
These humorous breezes, just wild enough,
Bring laughs to my heart in a twilight of fluff.

Glances Between the Frames

In the frames on the wall, the memories peek,
A gnome with a grin, giving out a cheek.
He winks at the photo of a toddler in mid-sneeze,
A snapshot of laughter that brings me to knees.

A plant in the corner, with leaves like a grin,
Expecting my secrets, it wears a sly spin.
While I whisper my quirks to the cat on the rug,
She rolls her green eyes with a big, furry shrug.

The clock ticks away with a rhythm so grand,
It's lost in the giggles, as time slips like sand.
Each second performs in a silly ballet,
I can't help but dance in a comical way.

These glimpses remind me of life in a spark,
Where laughter's the brushstrokes painting the dark.
With each silly glance, I welcome the cheer,
In this playful gallery, I hold dear.

Whispers Kissed by the Breeze

A squirrel with shades, so cool and bright,
He dances on branches, a comical sight.
The curtains sway softly, a gentle embrace,
As I giggle at nature, lost in her grace.

The wind tells secrets, all giggles and space,
While flowers do tango, a colorful chase.
I ponder the whispers that drift through the air,
With a wink and a nod, they tug at my hair.

A bird sings a tune, with a twist and a cheer,
And I can't help but chuckle, it's joy that I hear.
The bees plot a heist, a raucous parade,
In this wacky ballet, laughter won't fade.

So here I am, peeking, a witness to glee,
This lively affair, oh, the antics I see.
With nature as partner, a comic delight,
I share in the laughter, my heart feels so light.

Nature's Call from the Outside

The grass shouts 'hello!' with a tickle and tease,
While ants form a line like they own the whole breeze.
A cat in a hat seems to plot a retreat,
With a wise little smirk, he can't feel his feet.

The trees whisper jokes that they share with the sky,
The clouds play pranks, like they're floating on high.
A dog tries to howl but ends up a bark,
In this circus of life, it's a suspenseful lark.

The flowers are gossiping, red-faced with glee,
They chat with the sun, so carefree and free.
Each critter conspires in this madcap parade,
The garden's alive with the fun that we've made.

From soft, rolling laughter to giggles that bloom,
I can't help but chuckle while stuck in my room.
Nature's a comedian, sharing her jest,
I'm stealing her punchlines – oh, isn't it best?

Glimmers of Dawn

The sun peeks in, with a sleepy yawn,
While curtains dance wildly, a whimsical dawn.
My dreams still linger, like soap bubbles bright,
Pop! goes the morning, a hilarious sight.

The rooster crows loud, like he's in a play,
While the cat rolls her eyes, 'not another day!'
The coffee pot sputters, with a hiss and a puff,
As I sip on my brew, it's not nearly enough.

The flowers stretch tall, like they've just had a dream,
In this morning ballet, all things are supreme.
The birds start their chorus, a cacophony sweet,
With each chirp and chirr, a joyful heartbeat.

So here in my sanctuary, laughter does rise,
As I watch the world wake with such goofy guise.
A spectacle painted in gold and in pink,
In this glorious mess, it's the joy that I think.

Echoes Beyond the Glass

A dog with a woof and a wiggle so spry,
Hiccups and flops like a clown in the sky.
The neighbors are grilling, the smoke drifts with flair,
While sauces and laughter tumble through the air.

The wind chimes are giggling, so light on their strings,
Chiming in notes only nature can sing.
A toddler trips over his own little feet,
As I chuckle and cringe at his audacious feat.

The leaves play their games, a rustle and roll,
As squirrels judge each other, hippos in shoals.
A strange kind of circus, this life outside here,
And I can't help but laugh with a giggle or cheer.

So whisper your secrets, oh life full of jest,
In the laughter I'm caught; it's the world at its best.
These echoes of joy dance around in my head,
In this whimsical scene, all worries have fled.

The Space Between Dreams and Reality

In twilight's glow, my socks take flight,
A flying carpet of cotton delight.
The bed's a ship on sheets of white,
My dreams set sail into the night.

Pillow fights with shadows that dance,
Tangled sheets, a whimsical chance.
I drift on waves, in a dreamlike trance,
While reality's pranks steal my glance.

The clock is a pirate, tick-tock in stealth,
Raiding my rest, hoarding my health.
Yet here in the chaos, I find my wealth,
In giggling hopes and sleep's sly stealth.

So if you peek in, beware the spree,
Of giggles and whispers, wild and free.
For in this realm, it's just you and me,
Laughing at life, as grand as can be.

Flickers of Forgotten Dreams

A sock puppet winks and dips a bow,
It tells me tales of the things I know.
The cat's a guardian, wise and low,
While I'm the hero of this nightly show.

Chasing my thoughts like butterflies bright,
I catch them in jars, oh, what a sight!
Each flicker's a laugh, a quirky light,
That dances and chuckles, then takes flight.

The moon's my partner in a silly waltz,
We spin through dreams, without a fault.
Unicorns prance, and the dragon vaults,
As I snicker and sigh at all my schmaltz.

So here in the night, I shall remain,
With laughter and whimsy, joy, and a grain.
No worries or woes, just a lighthearted gain,
In the winks of the night, it's all just playful rain.

Sunbeams on the Surface

Golden rays tickle my sleepy face,
Like a bright parade of daytime grace.
They make my bed a joyous place,
Where sunlight dances and dreams embrace.

The cat's on a mission, a stealthy thief,
Stealing warm spots, oh, what a brief!
While I laugh softly, seeking relief,
In this sunlit battle, my cheerful belief.

Cereal spills like treasure on the floor,
A crunchy carpet that I adore.
Each spoonful reminds me of times before,
When breakfast was laughter, who could ask for more?

So let the sunbeam play its game,
In a comical scene, nothing's the same.
As I rise with a chuckle, the day's now tame,
With joy and sunshine, I'll stake my claim.

Whispers of the Horizon

Behind the curtain, secrets abound,
Whispers of dreams are all around.
A talking clock with jokes profound,
Keeps me chuckling without a sound.

The window creaks, gossip from outside,
A parade of squirrels, my friends abide.
They scheme and scamper with playful pride,
In their antics, I find joy supplied.

With every breeze, the curtains sway,
They dance to tunes of the warm array.
I join in laughter, come what may,
In dreams and whispers, I find my way.

So peek into this world, come take a look,
It's filled with giggles, like a secret book.
For in this haven, with every nook,
Lies humor and joy, in every crook.

The Canvas of Nightfall

Stars start to twinkle, a cheeky show,
As curtains dance gently, putting on a glow.
A raccoon steals snacks, how rude and spry,
I muse from my perch, the king of the sly.

Moths perform ballet, drawn to the light,
While shadows play tag, giving me a fright.
My socks go missing, a mystery today,
Leaving me puzzled in a comical way.

Reality Beyond the Inlet

In the twilight hour, the oddities roam,
As a squirrel throws acorns, claiming my home.
The moon grins wide, as if in on a joke,
And laughter erupts from a slumbering oak.

I spot a lost cat, dressed like a sage,
Peering at me like he's turned a new page.
With antics aplenty, they craft a delight,
In this wacky world, every evening's a riot.

Framed by Night's Caress

A dog howls loudly, serenading the dark,
While crickets tap dance, ignited by spark.
Laughter erupts as a bird tries to sing,
It's a horrible sound, yet joy it brings.

The fence creaks and groans, like it's telling tales,
Of wild nighttime adventures and grand epic fails.
As ghosts of past socks chase each other in flight,
This delightful chaos spills well into the night.

Lantern of Possibilities

The lantern swings gently, lighting the scene,
As a raccoon tiptoes, all sneaky and keen.
He trips over leaves, a clumsy display,
While I chuckle softly at his grand ballet.

The wind starts to giggle, a playful breeze,
Tickling the branches, coaxing leaves from trees.
It's a comedy show, written by the stars,
As I sip my cocoa, counting the bizarre.

A Footstep into Tomorrow

A sock misplaced, a shoe askew,
My pet cat sprawls in a sunbeam's hue.
The clock ticks loud, but I just sit tight,
Tomorrow calls, but I sleep through the night.

A pancake dance on the kitchen floor,
Flour on my nose, oh what a chore!
Tickling the air with laughter and grace,
As I twirl round in my breakfast space.

A leap of faith off the bed, oh dear!
Landing on teddy, my fuzzy frontier.
The day is bright, and my dreams are large,
On this wild ride, I'm ready to charge!

So bring on the mischief and giggles galore,
With each little blunder, I can't help but roar.
Life's a circus, just look at the show,
Every new misstep, a chance to grow!

Moments Caught in Time

A sandwich waits, but who takes the prize?
The dog will pounce with glimmering eyes.
The laundry spins, a tumble of fun,
As socks escape like a fast little run.

With breadcrumbs scattered like treasure on floors,
I chase the sounds of tiny paws' roars.
Watching the antics of life unfold,
Each silly moment, a story retold.

A tickle from a feather, a giggle so loud,
As I hide behind pillows, feeling quite proud.
A chase in the sunshine, let's take a wild ride,
In this playground world, let's put worries aside!

Moments like bubbles that shimmer and gleam,
Pop! What a mess, oh what a dream!
Life's like a carnival, spinning 'round bright,
In steadfast laughter, we find our delight.

Secrets Whispered in Light

A glow in the darkness, a flickering flame,
The ice cream stash calls out by name.
With cookies in hand, my heart starts to race,
Whispers of flavor in this sweet secret place.

The curtains rustle with tales to be told,
Of midnight snacks, bravely bold.
Under the covers, a disco of dreams,
As giggles escape like mischievous streams.

A secret fort made of cushions and sheets,
Where kings and queens share their favorite treats.
A lamp casts shadows, a castle's grand walls,
In this laughter-filled realm, adventure enthralls.

So let's keep it hush, just between us two,
These little night whispers, our own silly crew.
In the glow of the moon, let our hearts take flight,
For in this sweet secret, we find our delight!

The Storylines of Shifting Shadows

In the corner a shadow begins to dance,
A tale of whimsy, given a chance.
With a playful leap, it twirls on the wall,
Chasing the light till it stumbles and falls.

Whispers of silliness bait the air,
Unfolding the secrets of a mischievous dare.
When slippers take flight on a midnight glide,
And stuffed bears gather for stories inside.

Chasing the giggles, those laughing shapes change,
As bedtime approaches, the night feels strange.
A twist here, a turn there, the shadows collide,
In the margin of night, the wild thoughts abide.

Stories keep twisting as dreams come alive,
In the tapestry woven where giggles thrive.
With shadows as sketches, we play and explore,
Through the laughter, our imaginations soar!

The World Beyond the Tapestry

A cat sits perched, with curious glee,
Watching the world, as wild as can be.
Birds in a dance, the squirrels in flight,
It's a circus performance, oh what a sight!

Neighbors parade in their mismatched socks,
While a dog in the yard digs up old rocks.
The mailman's a hero, delivering cheer,
As the sun waves goodbye, it's all coming clear.

From laughter to chaos, peeking with zest,
The world's an odd stage, and I'm quite the guest.
Mom's yelling dinner, don't miss the fun,
Yet here I remain, for the show's just begun!

In every distraction, a sparkle, a scheme,
Life through the curtain—oh, what a dream!
With humor in chaos, and joy in the mess,
I giggle and chuckle; I couldn't care less.

Twilight's Gaze

As shadows stretch long, what news do they bring?
Dad's hunting for snacks, oh let the fun swing!
The curtains part softly, a grand reveal,
A parade of night critters with zero appeal!

Frogs in the pond share their ribbiting tales,
While crickets complain about gusty gales.
With my trusty flashlight, I'm ready for fright,
Or perhaps a surprise, in the shroud of the night!

There's Alice the raccoon, quite chubby and spry,
She wobbles like jelly, oh my, oh my!
The moon sends its smiles, keeping time with the fun,
While I giggle along, oh, how moonlight can run!

Through all the mischief and playful delight,
The world is a canvas in fading twilight.
Each glance out the peak brings some laughter anew,
Under stars that are sparkling, like morning dew.

A Window to the Infinite

What lies beyond? A caboodle of bliss,
Each glimpse a treasure, nothing amiss.
A bird with odd hairdos, doing a dance,
And that odd planter; did it have a chance?

A bobblehead mailbox, it grins with flair,
While the hedgehog in socks eats a sweet pear.
As gnomes hold a conference by bright garden lights,
And moonbeams throw glitter on fantastical sights!

A squirrel with ambitions, a scheme so grand,
Plans to steal acorns, the best in the land.
With giggles and chuckles, it hops to each feat,
A mission of mischief, a comedic repeat!

Through this portal of laughter, life takes its twist,
Every view a spectacle, none to be missed.
I can't help but chuckle, with joy in my heart,
For the world is a stage, and we all play a part!

The Heartbeat of Nightfall

As the day softly wanes, the fun's just begun,
A parade of quirks under the setting sun.
Neighbors in costume, what a sight to behold,
As laughter erupts, and stories unfold!

The clock strikes eight, it's party-time buzz,
While cats chase their tails, and the dog starts to fuzz.
With twinkling lights on the porch, what a show,
As owls hoot a rhythm, just letting it flow!

A raccoon in a tutu joins the dance floor,
While the wooden garden gnome boogies some more!
The wind starts to giggle, running through trees,
It's a night full of fun, with an air of great tease.

So here at my window, I peer through with glee,
To the heartbeat of nightfall, wild and free.
With creatures a-buzz, causing mayhem and joy,
It's a whimsical world, my own little ploy!

www.ingramcontent.com/pod-product-compliance
Lightning Source LLC
Chambersburg PA
CBHW070004300426
43661CB00141B/204